CHARTED PEASANT DESIGNS FROM SAXON TRANSYLVANIA

CHARTED PEASANT DESIGNS
FROM SAXON TRANSYLVANIA

Edited and Introduced by
HEINZ EDGAR KIEWE

DOVER PUBLICATIONS, INC., NEW YORK

My great thanks are due to:

Prof. Friedrich Volbach, late keeper of the Museo Sacro of the Vatican Museum in Rome, the late Prof. Samuel Krauss, Cambridge, and Prof. Robert Eisler, Oxford.

Thanks to my friends Dr. Bruno Fuerst, Oxford, the Art Historian, and Dr. Cecil Roth, the great Historian, both of whom endeavoured through many years to prune and again to enrich my views—

And to Maria Madalena de Gagigal e Silva, Conservator of the Museu de Arte Popular, Lisbon, who showed me on hand of the beautiful display of Portuguese Indian folkcarving—the strange migration of the "Tree of Life", the fountain head that nourished man's mind since primordial days.

HEINZ EDGAR KIEWE, OXFORD, 1962

Bibliographical Note

This Dover edition, first published in 1977, is an unabridged republication of the work originally published in Germany in 1964 under the title *Folk Cross-Stitch Design*. It is reprinted by special arrangement with the original publisher, Hans Meschendörfer, Schlesierstrasse 44/I, D-8000 Munich 80, Germany.

DOVER *Pictorial Archive* SERIES

International Standard Book Number
ISBN-13: 978-0-486-23425-0
ISBN-10: 0-486-23425-8

Manufactured in the United States by LSC Communications
23425815   2017
www.doverpublications.com

INTRODUCTION

The Cross stitch designs of the Transylvanian Saxons are amongst the most remarkable and beautiful abstract Folkembroideries in existence. Collected by EMIL SIGERUS in Edwardian days, at times when the Saxons' country belonged to the Austro-Hungarian Empire, they represent a unique collection of Folklore designs that echo those of mediaeval and Romanesque days. Their prototypes,—thanks to the strange fossilization of "counted" designs,—can be traced back to Norman Sicily of the 12th century when Muslim, Jewish and Christian textile craftsmen in peaceful cooperation created the base for abstract European symbols and design under King Frederick II in precious silkweaves. Some prototypes even come from earlier sources,—from the Egypt of the Coptic weavers and the Hellenistic tapestry weavers who had the Bible translated into Greek, the SEPTUAGINTA (about 270 before our era) and who wove the first tapestries of the Genesis at Alexandria.

Art historians still wonder why some Folk designs are practically the same in Morocco of North Africa, in Spain, Sardinia, Assisi of Italy and on the Greek Isles as with the Saxons' Roumanian neighbours. Indeed this proves that too little notice has been taken in art research,—of the easiest way of how patterns travelled and migrated in olden times, namely by embroidered and woven textiles. The Phoenicians, e.g., the traders of the Damasque of Damascus, the Gauze of Gaza, the purple silks from Tyre and the famous embroideries and woven cloth of Greater Syria, in their time spread them through agencies all around the Mediterranean—at the African as well as at the European coast, till the days of Alexander the Great. With their designs—especially the "Tree of Life"—the Phoenicians traded the stories and the religious ideas of the Eastern Mediterranean, the legend of the invisible God that was represented by a tree of life, by a Fountain of life and peacocks who stood on earth for the Cherubim and sacrificed to HIM, even animals.

Foreign corn in foreign lands, the cross stitch designs charted and published in this book were embroidered by Saxon women of Transylvania. They tell the story of mediaeval colonists of Western Europe whom fate had thrust into a strange Eastern Europe, the world of the Balcan of the 12th century. Since then Saxons lived for centuries on a plateau called Transylvania, once Hungarian, then Austrian and now Roumanian. They were walled in by 6000 feet heights of Carpathian mountains and by the Transylvanian Alps. They lived betwixt peasants of many origins, religions and nations, and the Roumanian people, (the ancient Thracians and Dacians of Roman history) grouped round them in a great circle. They tilled the soil next to Hungarians—who invaded as Magyars the country from the Far East 1000 years ago, with the Szeklers, a brother people of the Magyars, with the Ruthenians and the many who had a native mother and a Turkish invader as father. In a disunited league of nations,—some faithful to Greek Orthodoxy, some to Roman Catholicism,—these Saxon colonists lived an uneasy life for generations, yet they remained one community. Perhaps the Saxons felt that their progressive Protestantism, and their belief in science, made them the image of the free Western people in an Eastern Balcan that was freed from slavery or serfdom only some 100 years ago. Many of these Saxons are living today as expellees in Western Germany and, owing to their assistance, the new edition of this unique collection has been made possible.

What makes these Saxons or, rather, their women, remarkable is the re-discovered calligraphic evidence that, in a vacuum of their own choice, they kept a romantic bond with their country, with the fairy stories of their homeland, with its taste and love for precision, and the tradition of the Frank culture of Charlemagne reborn during the Renaissance.

Many of the designs in this book are precious witnesses of a sea of diverse religious waves that stirred symbols and signs from the Holy Lands to Western Europe, by trade winds, with crusaders, pilgrims, and with itinerant craftsmen and designers.

Some of the patterns printed on the pages, descend from a lineage dating back to periods long before our era; somehow they remained alive in Transylvania though they had been lost in Western Europe and the countries of the Eastern Mediterranean. Blossoming as strange blends of superstition and religion, some were welded by a precision in taste and with deep respect for the iconoclastic biblical laws of almost 3500 years. A few still incorporate today the geometrical speculations of Hebrewism, a great number express the sincere devotion of Catholicism, while others show delight in the liberating ideas of Protestantism. Many were formed by a generous inspiration of Islam design, Islam design that gave Europe the form in art and embroidery in the Middle Ages.

Independent of the magnificent heirlooms reported, the Saxon embroiderers seem to have exercised a very personal taste in the use of them all by having a sort of hygienic flair for white washed linen,—long before this fancy was selected as a clinical ideal in later ages. Such Puritan pride of whiteness laced with cross stitch design in monochrome blue or cherry red or black on a clear white foil is in striking difference to the polychromous gaiety of the cheerful, extrovert display of local Roumanian embroidery,—worked in bright coloured wools, silk metalthreads on leather or wool or bright coarse linen. Indeed the Saxon's women's "hygienic apron" must have looked like a sort of female heraldic device to the Balcan peasant neighbours.

There seems a sophistication even in the Saxon females' precision of stitch—in earlier work,—alike on both sides of the linen in pattern and clearness. Which way Saxon women held their needles for cross-stitch: horizontally or vertically or on the bias,—the needle aimed "towards the heart",—some source explain romantically.

In contrast to this Western method Roumanian embroiderers point their needles outward—the same way as we stitch with a sacking needle outwards, probably as a preventive to wounding ourselves should the needle pass abruptly through heavy material.

The Quaternity of the Cross

Hans Wuehr in his German introduction to this volume feels "that the beauty of the motifs collected and reproduced by Sigerus is founded on the capability to throw rays out in symmetry and coordination and make them form the important part of form and figure. Symmetry", he says, "is the beginning of the tradition of the Lord's creation on the first day, creation that brought order into the chaos of the world by setting a centre—dividing light and darkness, distributing—to a left and to a right. And above against underneath, Cherubim against Lucifer. All ceremonials," he concludes, "which express something Holy, ceremonies or feasts, are happening in the aspect of symmetry whether it be the spheric order of the stars, the majestas domini, the shrine of the altar, the religious service, the church façade or the rose window [that orientates the prayer towards Jerusalem],—the seal and symbols of religious orders or heraldry."

"Motives in Processions"

"In festivities it is the line, the balanced rhythmic order forming an endless procession or a continuous repetition towards all sides. Thus a motif is repeated like a gay singsong or like a monotonous formula of a liturgy, repeating itself endlessly and freezing in repetition.

"There are—cast in procession—the names of the first-born, the birthdays, the wedding and the end. Such-like follows the pattern of an embroidery border, so hang the plates, the tankards and the cups on the dresser in a peasant home. All processions are symbols of a moral, they should be understood as a parable."

When the Cross is used as a base of an embroidery design it seems remarkable that crosses fitting in a square are only used, not crosses of the elongated type—the ancient T on which Jesus is being crucified in art through all centuries although none of the art works earlier than the 7th century ever shows it in this way. Siebenbürger embroidery uses the Greek Cross only and the St. Andrew's cross combined—in short the Quaternity Cross.

Visiting by chance Amalfi and Patras while writing down this script, the writer observed local monuments which confirm the X oblique, even-armed length of the cross on which the Greeks martyred St. Andrew at Patras before the body was taken to Scotland in the 8th century. Are the traditions of folk-embroidery, then, closer to the archetype of the true cross than the elongated Gothic crosses of European painters? Was, then, the Greek Orthodox Church more resistant to artistic alterations, to elongated forms—so much more fitting to North European taste than to the dynamic Eastern Mediterranean style of weaving and carving? Horizontal and oblique, so was the Quaternity Cross that came as Star of Bethlehem from the Holy Land, a symbol recognized and called such by members of the three great monotheistic religions of the Holy Land. In craft it was the all pervading sign, used by all Christians and Muslims to this day in textile craft. It was the symbol of orientation used on early compass cards—a quaternity cross pointing to Jerusalem and thus to the East—where the light comes from.

It is a debatable point when the Saxon embroiderers started to use their lovely Quaternity star (crosses). Did they bring them from their Francon homes in the 12th century, did they copy them from the model books of the 16th century, or absorb them from the Greek Orthodox Church patterns surrounding them? Or were they taken from carpet designs produced by members of the Armenian faith, who in unison with the Syriac and Coptic Church kept strictly to the iconoclastic laws of Moses? Was this quaternity cross the first cross ever fashioned on textiles by early Christians?

Like pictures in a kaleidoscope, the beautiful variations of Saxon star crosses pass our wondering eyes. They are like ancient ideograms we cannot yet read. Do they tell of local traditions, emotional legends, do they tell us of faith or superstition,—of which mankind was never free,—or are they a deep bond of a village for an ancient sign or symbol formed in forgotten days long before the idea of the Trinity was throught of?

The Saxon Folk cross-stitch designs collected by Emil Sigerus may be of varied origin. They may be new copies, recopied from old copies or prototypes that have been lost long ago. But with their traditions in craft intact—they form a phantastique legend of the many religious moods of Europe and the lands round the Mediterranean during 2000 years and longer. Though Francon heirlooms from the Rhine formalized in Eastern Europe, many originated at the fountain of our civilization–the Greater Syria and Greece where much abstract Folk design has died partly by the ideas and by the hands of Western Europe that had been nursed by these civilizations.

Heinz Edgar Kiewe

HISTORICAL ABSTRACT
IMPORTANT TO THE HISTORY OF FOLK CROSS STITCH DESIGNS

c. 1920   The known world believes in gods. (Polytheism) Call of Abraham. He smashed his father's idols.

c. 1495   Moses led the Israelites out of Egypt. Ten Commandments. Iconoclastic Law against figurative art, replacement of idols by abstract designs. (Monotheism)
Erection of an abstract "brazen serpent" (Caduceus-first symbol of social medicine) by Moses. Bezalel, first craftsmen in abstract art mentioned historically by name, uses SHBZ – "Weave in chequer" (geometric, bird's eye weave), prototype of the "Holy Chequer" ornament.

1 st. century   "Paul leaves Athens and travels to Corinth. He meets Aquila and Priscilla and because he was of the same trade, he made his home with them, and they carried on business together, they were tent makers" (Weavers of Kelim carpets of abstract design).

325–381   Trinity Athanasius. Father of Orthodoxy, Bishop of Alexandria. Beginning of symbolical representation of the Trinity in Christian abstract art.

380   Byzantine style, "Non-realistic, almost abstract, with no depth of perspective."

451   Members of the Coptic, Syriac and Armenian Church form an iconoclastic movement.

726–843   Dispute on iconoclasm in religious worship in churches of the East.

The Iconoclast' Controversy, Turning on the Propriety of Representing the Deity in Human Form, Disturbed the Byzantine Empire Throughout the Eighth and Ninth Century

  First representations of Jesu crucified (Figurative art).

800   Charlemagne decrees that not only flax and wool, but also "Waisdo, vermiculo, varentia", that is woad, cochineal dye and madder, should be produced. (43rd chapter of the administracion of his land.)

960   Magyars invade Hungary from Central Asia and introduce Asian/Chinese folk embroidery designs in Balcan countries.

1194–1250   Frederic II, King of Sicily, first European-minded Emperor of West Europe. Under his guidance craftsmen of Muslim, Christian and Jewish faith create the basis of European Romanesque art at Palermo (Sicily) in design woven in precious silks.

1141–1161   Migration of "Saxons" from the Mosel, Rhine and Lower Saxony to Transylvania under Geysa II of Hungary.

1211–1225   The Knights Templar stay in Transylvania and make known, probably to the Saxons, religious textile designs from Sicily and Venice.

2nd half 13th. century   Poet Wolfram von Eschenbach praises the precious Lendel silk fabrics of Ratisbon (Regensburg-on-the Danube). Patterns of these fabrics "which followed closely the Venetian style" (O. V. Falke) became, no doubt, the prototype of Transylvanian cross stitch designs.

1370   Highest affluency of Transylvanian Saxons. 19 Guilds and 25 crafts in existence. Saxon merchants travel in armed caravans to Constantinople (Byzanz), to the Aegean and Adriatic seas and to the "Golden Hordes" north of the Black Sea.

1400   Start of Turkish invasions.

1438   Beginning of enforced school system in Saxon Transylvania.

1498–1549   Johannes Honterus: Saxons accept and join united Lutheran Reformation.

1524   Some geometric patterns appear as woodcuts in the "Modebooks of counted patterns" of
Schoensperger (Zwickau, Saxony), 1524
Peter Quentel (Cologne), 1527
Tagliente (Venice), 1527
Zoppino (Venice), 1529
Andreas Vavassore (Venice), 1530
Celle and Coste (Lyons), 1537
Johann Sibmacher (Nuremberg), 1597
Rosina Helena Fuerst (Nuremberg), 1660.

1686–1918   Transylvania under Austrian monarchy.

1717–1780   Maria-Theresia of Austria.
Many Lutheran reformed Austrians, persecuted for their faith, leave the lands of the Alps and join the Saxons of Transylvania.
Probably beginning of the "Flowery style" of Folk Cross Stitch.

1754   Monthly post coach between Vienna and Transylvania.

1919   Transylvania incorporated in Roumania.

NOTES TO PLATES
THEIR PROBABLE ORIGINS, DATES, AND USE OF PATTERNS

PLATE I: 1-4. PILLOWS. Hermannstädter Kreis

1) Syrian scroll: Poppies *(17th century)*
   Prototype: Rosina Helena Fürst, Nuremberg, Modelbuch 1660

2) Woven braid pattern *(16th century)*

3) "Peacock of paradise carnation tree of Life"
   Two Dimensional tapestry weave
   Pattern found also on Greek Isles and Sardinia (16th century)

See plate I (3)
THE TREE (FOUNTAIN) OF LIFE. 17/18 th century embroidery Azemour (Maroc) of Phoenician Prototype

4) The lion cross with a border of "S" Symbols of health (caducaeus of medicine)★
   Norman Sicilian (11th century)
   (see also 4, 19, 47, 70, 79)

PLATE II: 5-9. PILLOWS. Heltau 1678

5) Carnation border
   Shamrock (woven braid) pattern *(18th century)*

6) (Good) "Shepherds staff" pattern *(Byzantine style)*

7) Holbein stitch border (fleur de lys)
   Star braid pattern *(16th century)*

8) Syrian scroll with musk pattern *(18th century)*

9) Holbein stitch border
   Star (cross) braid pattern *(Byzantine style)*

★ *S = Symbol of brazen serpent of the Bible (Caduceus)*
The serpent was revered by the Phoenicians and Egyptians as a symbol of regeneration and the renewal of life. M. H. Farbridge suggests that the power attributed to the brazen serpent in the Bible is "based on the fact that the serpent in the Bible was regarded amongst the Hebrews as a symbol of renewed energy and vigour. The brazen serpent was placed high upon a pole to remind the person bitten by the snake that the God of Heaven was the great healer of disease, and that it is to HIM that the people must look for a sure." It became thus the first emblem of social medicine historically reported.

★★ *Quaternity*
Being four; set of four persons (esp. of the God head in contrast to *Trinity*) (F. LL Quaternitas).
Quaternity—"the four corners of the earth and the four winds of heaven". (Dan. VII.2.)

PLATE III: 10-12. PILLOWS. Leschkirch

10) Fairy queen (Mary) and (Lilytree) House spirits (Cherubim) *Tree of life Fountain of life (16th century)*

11) Falconeering
    Falconer with saxon cap
    Prototype: Augsburg or South Tyrol (first half 16th century)

12) Peacocktail feather star (Cross) *(Byzantine style)*

See plate III (12)
THE LILY CROSS. Braid from Cologne 14/15 th century

PLATE IV: 13-15. PILLOWS. Hermannstädter Kreis

13) Border of passion flowers centre "Chinese cloud" –
    Probably brought from Asia to Hungary by Magyars in 960
    Prototype Rosina Helena Fürst, Nuremberg, Modelbuch 1660

14) Star (cross) in Laurels holy salver border
    Biedermeier *(early 19th century)*

15) Lily of the valley border
    (Diagonal = persian) prototype *18th century*
    Star of Bethlehem woven braid pattern "The quaternity cross"★★ *(Earliest Christian sign)*

PLATE V: 16-20. PILLOWS. Hermannstädter Kreis

16) King's fallen crown (Hungary's 1686?) *(17th century)*

17) Peacock-fountain of life
    Trefoil (Shamrock) braid pattern *(18th century)*

18) "Fleur de lys" border
    Procession of (italian?) stags tree of life *(16th century)*

19) Peacocks and the trinity of paradise
    Michaelmas daisy (aster grandiflora)
    "S" scroll, symbol of social medicine
    (see no. 4, 47, 70, 79)
    (see Moses' brazen serpent of exodus)
    Prototype: Giovanni Ostaus, Venice, pattern LXX 1561 A.D.

20) Queen of heart and snapdragons *(18th century)*

PLATE VI: 21. BEDSPREAD, Jaad; 22. TABLECLOTH, Minarken; 23. BESPREAD, Jaad; 24. PILLOW, Peschendorf; 25. BEDSPREAD, Wallendorf; 26. TABLECLOTH, Minarken; 27. BEDSPREAD, Wallendorf; 28. PILLOW, Meschendorf

21) Asters and roman ornament *(19th century)*
22) Tulip star (cross) *(18th century)*
    Tulip (emblem of the chalice, holy grail, the woman)
23) Trinity braid* *(18th century)*
24) Star (cross) between acanthus branches (christian arab, Holy land)
    (Fern, palm, pine?) (See related pattern 53, 32)
25) Byzantine star (cross) anchor cross of the king of kings
    Greek P = (R) = Rex *(17th century)*
    (see also no. 50)
26) Syrian scroll *(18th century)*
27) Woven braid border *(18th century)*
28) Snapdragon (art nouveau) *(20th century)*

PLATE VII: 29. PILLOW, Nadesch; 30, 31. PILLOW, Oberneudorf

29) Cross in eternity after byzantine style *(19th century design)*
30) Birdseye
    Star cross with acanthus leaves. Ramsheads = symbol of perseverance. Biedermeier (neo classicism)
    (early 19th century)
31) Feather of peacock star (cross) of paradise with acanthus branch *(18th century)*

See plate VII (31)
THE QUATER-
NITY ROSE.
Romanesque half-silk tissue Ratisbone 13th century

PLATE VIII: 32. PILLOW, Deutsch-Pien; 33, 34. TOWELS, Grosskockler Kreis; 35. PILLOW, Minarken

32) Tree of life border with holy salver
    (Prototype: Christian Arab Ramallah, Holy Land)
    (See similar style of diffusion No. 24)
    Pomegranate cross
    Empire (Biedermeier) *(early 19th century)*

See plate VIII (32)
THE TULIP
CROSS. Byzantine
7th-11th century

33) Lily of the valley border
    Procession of 14th century peacocks
    Harts** (stags) and trinity (fleur de lys)
35) "You are my vine"*** (inhabited Syrian scroll)
    (18th century)

PLATE IX: 36–41. PILLOWS. Burzenland

36) Border holy oil salvers (inhabited Syrian scroll)
    Peacock tail star (crosses) acorn   Patterns
    (18th century)
37) Greek star (cross) after Byzantine prototype *(18th century)*
38) Star of lilies (symbol of Mary, and symbol of purity)
    (18th century)
39) Holbein stitch border *(16th century)*
40) Woven braid border, peasant style *(16th century)*
41) Angels at the gate of paradise (Trinity of Paradise)
    (18th century)

PLATE X: 42. PILLOW, Burzenland; 43. PILLOW, Neppendorf; 44–46. PILLOWS, Burzenland

42) Woven braid pattern (Byzantine) *(16th century)*
43) Star of Bethlehem tree of life****
    Inhabited Syrian scroll *(18th century)*

---

* Trinity
Being three; group of three; the trinity—union of three persons (father, son, holy spirit) in one god head, doctrine of his, whence trinitarian; symbolical representation of the trinity in art and folk craft.

** Harts
Isaiah 35. 6, reads: "Then shall the lame man leap as an hart . . .,"

*** Vine
Psalm LXXX. 9. had a deep meaning for the Saxon colonists:
  9) "Thou didst pluck up a vine out of Egypt;
     Thou didst drive out the nations, and didst plant it."
  10) "Thou didst clear a place before it,
     And it took deep root, and filled the land."

**** Tree of Life
Tree of life, the, was like a vine (some say a palm). The Babylonian word for "wine" means "drink of life", and the word for vine means "tree of the drink of life". We know that the Babylonians made wine from the palm as well as the vine. The Hebrews probably regarded "the tree of life" as having been a vine. So in the New Testament "I am the vine".
Psalm 92.14
  14) "Planted in the house of the Lord,
     They shall flourish in the courts of our God"
  15) "They shall still bring forth fruit in old age
     They shall be full of sap and richness"

44) Lily of the trinity
   Inhabited Syrian scroll *(18th century)*

45) Thistle cross *(18th century)*

PLATE XI: 47. PILLOW, Minarken; 48. TABLECLOTH
Minarken; 49, 50. TABLECLOTHS, Talmesch;
51. SHIRT, Jaad; 52. PILLOW, Minarken

47) Holy candelabra protected by cherubim (symbolising
   wisdom)
   "S" = Symbol of health (Brazen Serpent)
   (see also 4, 19, 70, 79)

48) Tulip with "Running dog" border (Roman Ornament)
   (19th century)

49) Trinity of the 4 winds *(19th century)*

50) Cross of the king of kings (P)
   (see also No. 25)

51) Inhabited Syrian scroll (braid)

52) Tree of life growing from the flowering heart
   (19th century)
   Flowers: True star of Bethlehem (Ornithogalum
   umbellatum) and cornflower (Centaurea ragusina)

PLATE XII: 53, 54. TOWELS, Hermannstädter Kreis
55. PILLOW, Hermannstädter Kreis
56. APRON, Hermannstädter Kreis

53) Pine tree of life with the trinity
   Symbol of eternity
   (see related pattern, 24, 32)

54) Resurrection
   Easter hare (German symbol of easter) or donkey
   Style found in tapestry woven carpets,
   Aquila (Abruzzi), Italy

55) "The wild horses of the fiery invaders"
   *Prototype: Guesttowel, workrooms der Velman, Augsburg
   (about 1460)*
   Serpent symbol on tree of life
   (Symbol of Wisdom and terrestial sin)
   Border of asters *(17th century)*

56) Counter change braid (running dog) (Syrian?)

---

* *Cherubim:* A winged creature symbolic of the powers of nature
ministering to God. Cherubim were said to guard the entrance to the
Garden of Eden (Gen. III.24) overshadow the "mercy-seat" of the ark of
the covenant (Exod. XXV.18) and constitute the divine throne (2
Kings, XIX.15).

** *Birds,* eagles, raven, doves
"Birds are thoughts and the light of thoughts: Generally it is fantasies
and intuitive ideas that are represented thus (genii, angels)."
G. G. Jung, (Psychology and Alchemy).
Psalm XI,1: "In the Lord put I my trust; how say ye to my soul, flee
as a bird to your mountains."

PLATE XIII: 57. PILLOW, Minarken; 58. TOWEL,
Scholten; 59. PILLOW, Oberneudorf;
60. BEDSPREAD, Haschagen 1858; 61 TO-
WEL, Tartlau

57) Holbein stitch border
   Byzantine cross *(16th century)*

58) Persian griffins rampant *(16th century)*

59) Inhabited Syrian scroll *(19th century)*
   Bell flower   Biedermeier

60) "Cherubim (in birds form)* of the trinity"**
   Flowers: linum (flax)
   *Prototype: Giovanni Ostaus, Venice 1561, page LXX
   Reprinted from Schönsperger: Erstes Modellbuch,
   Zwickau: 1527/29*

See plate XIII (60)
Sicilian prototype 12th century

PLATE XIV: 62. PILLOW, Hamlesch; 63. TOWEL,
Hemlesch; 64. PILLOW, Minarken;
65. TOWEL, Rumes.

62) Corncob thieves (border)
   Double eagle and the fountain of life
   (Note the little devils)

63) Inhabited Syrian scroll
   Cross design in counter change   Biedermeier
   (19th century)

64) Tulip in trinity
   Ascension cloth *(19th century)*

65) Hunted stags at the fountain of life   Sophisticated
   (19th century)

PLATE XV: 66. TOWEL, Gergeschdorf; 67. PILLOW,
Stolzenburg; 68. PILLOW, Mettersdorf

66) Border
   Lamb and flag procession
   Stag on fountain of life
   (Sophisticated *19th century?*)

67) Inhabited Syrian scroll
   (Stars & crosses)   Biedermeier
   (19th century)

68) Hunted stag
   Chained to the tree of life poppy border (Rhoeas
   papaper)
   A variation of Sibmacher design *(17th century)*

9

PLATE XVI: 69. TOWEL, Bistritzer Kreis; 70. TOWEL, Urwegen; 71. PILLOW, Haschagen; 72. WALLHANGING, Oberneudorf

69) Procession of eagles (Sicilian *11th century?*)
(Representing St. John the Apostle)

70) Lions guarding the holy book (St. Marc)
(Old Testamentarian)

71) Syrian inhabited scroll
(Cornflower border) *(16th century)*

72) Dragons and the fountain of life
(Phoenician prototype) *(16th century model)*
"S" Border (health & Medicine)
(see also No. 4, 19, 47, 79) Outer border holy salver

PLATE XVII: 73. BEDSPREAD, Oberneudorf; 74. TOWEL, Honigberg; 75. TOWEL, Burzenland; 75. PILLOW, Meschendorf

73) Tree of life in paradise (Sicilian *11th century*)
Prototype

74) Puss in boots Art nouveau *(20th century)*

75) Tree and fountain of life Greek isles *(19th century)*

76) Lord' burial cloth*
Byzantine braid weave *(of early Christian origin)*

PLATE XVIII: 77. PILLOW, Schorsten; 78. TOWEL, Brenndorf; 79. TOWEL, Neppendorf

77) Wild rose trinity "Lady of the rose"
Rose is emblematic of love *(18th century)*
(see also 104, 115, 192)

78) Sweet pea star (cross)
Acanthus *(19th century)*

79) Border:
Procession of heavenly peacocks
centre "S" curve for health & medicine
(see also 4, 19, 47, 70)
Most sophisticated Siebenbürgen cross stitch design
(18th century)

PLATE XIX: TOWELS, Scholten; 82. PILLOW, Meschen; 83. TOWEL, Mergeln; 84. PILLOW, Thalheim; 85. PILLOW, Bistritz

80) Owls and oaks (art nouveau) *(20th century)*

81) Oriental diagonal "Swinging stars"

82) Acorn and "S" sign
(Strength & wisdom) *(16th century)*

83) Cherubims and acorn (faith & strength)

84) Pomegranate star (cross) (Byzantine style)
"Thy plants are an orchard of Pomegranates"
(Solomon 4:13) *(18th century model)*

85) Acanthus star (cross) *(16th century)*
Probably adapted from early Christian Sarcophagus
(see Elija Astigi) S. Cruz *(5th century)*

PLATE XX: 86. PILLOW, Hamlesch; 87. PILLOW, Reussmarkt; 88. WALLHANGING, Wallendorf; 89. TOWEL, Honigberg; 90. APRON, Minarken; 91. PILLOW, Stolzenburg

86) Tree of life (merry go round) *(19th century)*

87) Tree of life a trinity
Flower: Campanula carpatica *(19th century)*

88) Burning heart Sibmacher *(17th century prototype)*

89) Ringelreih *(19th century)*

89B) Running dog (Counter change) *(19th century)*

90) Centre: Skalli (Arabic)
= Sicilian eagles
(Sicilian *11th century prototype*)
Border: St. Andrew's cross
"S" sign (health and faith)

91) Trinity of bell flowers *(19th century)*

See plate XX (87)
after Sicilian Tree of Life 12th century

---

* The holy cloth: the holy chequer, the holy cross design.
Epithaphios trinos
EPITHPHIOI are ceremonial burial cloths. These fabrics are called in Greece (= MOURNING GRIEF) and in Slavic countries PLACHTCHANIZA (= BURIAL CLOTH). Both are often of highly artistic quality. In Greek Orthodox Churches —on Good Friday,— they are carried into the Nave of the church where they are rested to symbolize the HOLY GRAVE and remain there till Easter Nights.

Already the Old Testament mentions certain tapestry or rapport (repeat) weaves which represent lordly symbols expressed in designs of the Eastern Mediterranean "geometrical speculations". Bezalel,—first craftsman weaver ever mentioned in History, wove e.g., SHBZ, the Holy Chequer pattern, the "eyes of God".

Later to avoid mentioning God's ineffable name it was called "Birdseye weave", and is known under this name to handweavers even until today. With the coming of Christianity this biblical chequer pattern was replaced by a new symbol representing Christian thought and the first pattern, according to F. W. Volbach, late Keeper of the Museo Sacro of the Vatican, were apparently woven by the Christian community of Rome probably in the 1st century of our era.

To the veil of the Holy curtain in the temple, the swaddling band (or braia) of the new-born baby and those at burial ceremonies, the binders (see "religion" = derivation of re-ligare = to bind) wound round the scrolls of the law were fashioned symbolically with the new ideas expressed by the cross. The braid woven in cross symbols was used to cover the dish used for the bread of the eucharist—the Lord's supper, the robes were woven in the holy chequer of the cross and it is reported of the Church of Byzanz that the Evangeliar was wrapped with the crossbraid on Good Friday and carried in procession during the liturgy.

The origin of the cross ornated stola no doubt dates back to the same origin.

PLATE XXI: 92. TOWEL, Neustadt bei Schässburg; 93, 94. APRON, Halwelagen; 95. BED-SPREAD, Wallendorf

92) The mount and the Stars of Bethlehem *(18th century)*
93) Peacocks *(18th century)*
94) Tulip diagonals *(16th century)*
95) The hunted stag
Style found in tapestry woven carpets
At Aquila (Abruzzi), Italy *(end 17th century)*
The psalmist refers to it as the hart panting for the water of the brooks. Emblem of soul thirsting for baptism

PLATE XXII: 96. PILLOW, Scholten; 97. WALL-HANGING, Jaad; 98. WALLHANGING, Minarken; 99. PILLOW, Wallendorf

96) Snapdragon (Lion's mouth) (Antirrhinum)
Acorn Border and holy mount Phoenician influence
Peacocks and tree of life *(16th century)*
97) Margerite and Roman ornament *(19th century)*
98) Fuchsia (art nouveau) *(20th century)*
99) Sunflower border *(18th century)*
Roman ornament

PLATE XXIII: 100. TOWEL, Urwegen; 101. PILLOW, Arkeden; 102. PILLOW, Scholten; 103. TOWEL, Hermannstädter Kreis

100) The holy mount and the lily of the valley *(18th century)*
Chalice for balsam
Border: Syrian inhabited scroll acorn and St. Andrew's cross (strength and faith) *(16th century)*
101) Woven braid star (crosses)
Chequer pattern counterchange *(16th century)*
102) Peacocks and tree of life
(Sacrifice of flowers) *(16th century)*
(Phoenician prototype)
103) Corncob thieves *(18th century)*

PLATE XXIV: 104. PILLOW, Stolzenberg; 105. PILLOW, Petersdorf; 106. TOWEL, Haschagen; 107. TOWEL, Michelsberg; 108. PILLOW, Meschendorf; 109. PILLOW, Rumes.

See plate XXIV (104)
THE WOUNDED
HEART. After Johann
Sibmacher Nuremberg 1604

104) "Heart and ram" Love and Perseverance
Foundations of Tulip tree of life
(see also 77, 115, 192) Alpine flowery style?
(18th century)
105) Peacocks sacrificing fruit
From the tree of wisdom to fountain of life
(Phoenician Prototype) *(17th century model)*
106) Star of Bethlehem
Braid border
107) Dancing women
Sacrificing flowers to tree of life *(19th century)*
108) Quaternity peacock feather cross *(19th century)*
109) Flower border Art nouveau *(20th century)*

PLATE XXV: 110. TOWEL, Kleinbistritz; 111. TOWEL, Minarken; 112. TABLECLOTH, Wallendorf; 113. PILLOW, Neppendorf

110) Protecting the trinity *(20th century)*
111) Lily pattern *(18th century)*
112) Bethlehem star of the 4 winds Biedermeier
(19th century)
113) Raven on the tree of trinity (border)
Hazel nut motive Biedermeier
(early 19th century)

PLATE XXVI: 114. TABLECLOTH, Scholten; 115, 116. PILLOW, Michelsberg; 117. TO-WEL, Treppen; 118. PILLOW, Stein bei Reps; 119. PILLOW, Kleinscheuren; 120. PILLOW, Treppen

114) Shamrock (trinity) symbol
115) Flower motiv
(Turning into harvest dancer) *(18th century)*
(see also 77, 107, 192)
116) Wounded heart with the tree of life
The holy salver and mount *(19th century)*
117) Aster border *(18th century)*
118) Star of Bethlehem and the 4 Evangelists
also called 'Jerusalem Cross'
Fountain of life pattern after Byzantine braid motiv
(16th century)
119) Christmas rose (helleborus) border *(18th century)*

PLATE XXVII: 121. WALLHANGING (Stangentuch), Gross-Schogen; 122. PILLOW, Eibes-dorf; 123. PILLOW, Pretai; 124. TO-WEL, Treppen; 125. PILLOW, Treppen; WALLHANGING, Kelling

121) Floral tree of life *(19th century)*
122) Chevron repeat "Shields of the lord"
Emblematic of Gabriel the archangel who "stands in the presence of god" (St. Luke 1.19)
Norman/Sicilian prototype *(11th century)*

123) The lily or angel and St. Andrew's cross (cross saltire) Biedermeier
After Byzantine Prototype *(19th century)*
124) Fountains creating life *(19th century)*
125) Italian fountains of life
Rose border *(17th century)*
126) Demon (locust) pattern
Counterchange *(18th century)*
(see also 138)

PLATE XXVIII: 127. PILLOW, Stolzenburg; 128. TOWEL, Dobring; 129. PILLOW, Nepplendorf; 130. TOWEL, Halwelagen; 131. PILLOW, Oberneudorf; 132. TOWEL, Kelling; 133. TOWEL, Scholten; 134. PILLOW, Talmesch

127) The wise fox and the tree and fountain of life *(17th century)*
128) Double eagle (abstract)
(Emblem of Austria) *(19th century)*
129) Birds on the holy fountain *(18th century)*
130) Peacocks, border *(16th century)*
131) "Peacock of the quaternity star" procession *(18th century)*
132) Fruit border Biedermeier *(19th century)*
133) Peacock border Biedermeier *(19th century)*
134) St. Hubertus stag (with the cross)
(Sophisticated style 19th century)
135) Forest demon
Sacrificing water to the tree of live *(17th century)*

PLATE XXIX: 136. TABLECLOTH, Jaad; 137. PILLOW, Stolzenburg; 138. WALLHANGING (Stangentuch), Kelling

136) Byzantine tulip star
Other flowers: iris and snapdragon
(Model of 18th century)
137) 5 carnation (5 = symbol of Christianity)
(16th century)
138) Demon (locust) destroying life
Counterchange *(18th century)*
(see also 126)

PLATE XXX: 139. WALLHANGING, Gross-Schogen; 140. WALLHANGING, Treppen; 141. WALLHANGING, Minarken; 142. TOWEL, Treppen; 143. TOWEL, Neppendorf; 144. TOWEL, Treppen; 145. TOWEL, Hammersdorf

139) Tree of life (abstract) and Byzantine stars
(Sophisticated style 19th century)
(see also 156)

140) Tree of life Art nouveau *(20th century)*
141) Tulip tree of life *(18th century)*
142) Poppy flower (papaver) *(17th century)*
143) "Art nouveau" border *(20th century)*
144) Flower basket (Art nouveau) *(20th century)*
145) Goose walk border *(late 18th century)*

PLATE XXXI: 146. TOWEL, Neustadt bei Agnetheln; 147. BEDSPREAD, Reussmarkt; 148. PILLOW, Neppendorf; 149. PILLOW, Gross-Scheuern; 150. TOWEL, Schellenberg; 151. TOWEL, Michelsberg; 152. WALLHANGING, Talmesch; 153. TOWEL, Neppendorf; 154. PILLOW, Gross-Scheuern; 155. TOWEL, Neudorf

146) Raven's watch (Emblem of St. Paul of Thebes and symbol of Charlemagne)
(Sicilian 11th century prototype)
147) Tree of life of plants: Jacob's ladder (Polemonium) convolvulus and morning glory Biedermeier *(19th century)*
148) Doves and Sparrows *(18th century)*
Dove Psalm 55.7
—"Oh that I had wings like a dove!
Then I would fly away, and be at rest."
149) Heart, tree and cherubim)
(Love, hope and faith)
150) Syrian inhabited scroll
Carnation border *(16th century)*
151) Stags and the fleur de lys *(16th century)*
152) Pidgeon in procession
153) Holy Salver and acanthus
Christian Arab, Ramallah (Holy land) patterns
18th century)
154) The holy lamp (Emblem of John the Apostle)
(Sophisticated style 19th century)
155) Red robins *(18th century)*

PLATE XXXII: 156. WALLHANGING, Stolzenburg; 157. PILLOWS, Arbegen; 158. TOWEL, Hammersdorf; 159. PILLOWS, Thalheim; 160. WALLHANGING, Mettersdorf

156) The gates of paradise
The eyes of the lord (SHBZ = holy chequer pattern)
The holy candelabra
and peacocks of eternal life
(of Armenian? prototype) *(17th century)*
(see also 139)

157) Another version of the trinity of the heart
Christian Arab influence from Ramallah (Holy land?)
(18th century)

158) Wild strawberry border *(16th century)*

159) Symbols of eternity
Counterchange *(16th century)*

160) "Holy trinity of the winged cherubim"
Flower: Windflower (anemone coronaria)
(of 17th century prototype)

PLATE XXXIII: 161. PILLOW, Heidendorf; 162. PIL-
LOW, Kelling; 163. PILLOW, Girelsau

161) Woven braid "rapport"
Acanthus and peacock tail star (cross)
Columbine (aquilegia) border

162) "The lord's cloth"
Byzantine cross pattern weave *(14th century)*

163) Art nouveau border (honeysuckle) *(20th century)*

PLATE XXXIV: 164. PILLOW, Hahnbach; 165. TO-
WEL, Hammersdorf; 166. TABLE-
CLOTH, Tartlau; 167. PILLOW, Gross-
au; 168. PILLOW, Schönbirk; 169. PIL-
LOW, origin unknown

164) Lily of the valley border and holy mount pattern
Biedermeier *(19th century)*

165) Syrian scroll border
With the star of Bethlehem inserted *(19th century)*

166) Star of Bethlehem (quaternity cross)
Greek P = R = Rex = The Lord's sign in the cosmos
Flower (Chamomile = emblem of health)

167) Rose bud border

168) Winged hearts (or angel crosses)
In Syrian scroll *(late 18th century)*

169) Holy braid border:
The lord's eye (or birdseye lozenge pattern)
St. Andrew's cross (cross saltire)
and trefoil (shamrock) *(late 17th century)*

See plate XXXV
After Giovanni Andrea Vavassore, Venice 1530

PLATE XXXV: 170. PILLOW, Mühlbach

170) The dragon at the tree of life (see also No. 58)
(Emblem of St. Margaret of Antioch)
First published by Andreas Vavassore, 1530 Venice
Narcissus (bulbo codium) border
(Oriental diagonal)

PLATE XXXVI: 171. PILLOW, Kleinscheuern;
172. PILLOW, Hamlesch; 173. TABLE-
CLOTH, Tartlau; 174. TOWEL, Jaad;
175. APRON, Minarken; 176. PILLOW,
Michelsberg; 177. APRON, Minarken

171) The lord's cloth (quaternity crosses)
Emblem: Star of Bethlehem on the St. Andrew's cross
(cross saltire) *(16th century)*

172) Procession of stag and St. Hubert cross
(16th century) Italian

173) Byzantine pomegranate cross *(18th century)*

174) Counterchange border *(18th century)*

175) Norman Sicilian (Skalli) raven
(Emblem of St. Paul of Thebes and Charlemagne)
(11th century)

176) The vine border *(19th century)*

177) Trinity of Bethlehem star border *(18th century)*
(Quaternity cross)

PLATE XXXVII: 178. PILLOW, Scholten;
179. TABLECLOTH, Michelsberg;
180. TABLECLOTH, Wallendorf;
181. PILLOW, Eibesdorf

178) The star of Bethlehem braid with tree of life border
(18th century)

179) St. Andrew's star (cross saltire)
Christian Arab influence *(16th century)*

180) Flower wheel
Flower: Virgin's bower (clematis) *(18th century)*

181) Bethlehem star   Sophisticated style
In "Art nouveau" *(20th century)*

PLATE XXXVIII: 182. PILLOW, Frauendorf;
183. APRON, Mettersdorf;
184. APRON, Michelsberg; 185. PIL-
LOW, Hamlesch; 186. PILLOW, Stolzenburg

182) Peacock tail feather cross*
Weaving braid *(16th century)*

183) St. Andrew's cross border
(cross saltire) *(16th century)*

184) Windswept flower border *(18th century)*

185) Fleur de lys border *(19th century)*

186) The holy book and
The holy scroll of the trinity *(18th century)*

---

* As used in Sibmacher, Nuremberg, Model Book 1597.

13

See plate XXXVIII (182)
THE QUATERNITY CROSS. Coptic silks 6th century

PLATE XXXIX: 187. PILLOW, Bistritz; 188. APRON,
    Hahnbach; 189. TABLECLOTH, Ham-
    lesch; 190. PILLOW, Tartlau

187) The lord's cloth
 Weaving pattern:
 The lord's eyes (SHBZ = holy chequer pattern) and
 the star of Bethlehem (quaternity cross)
 Border: The oly linum (flax plant) with the shamrock
 of trinity
 "S" curve for caducaeus (Emblem of Health & Medicine) *(16th century model) Prototype Syrian holy land*
188) Roman "running dog" *(20th century style)*

189) Tree of life border Sophisticated style *(19th century)*
190) Tree of life
 Adaptation from Greek isles
 Art nouveau *(20th century)*
 Flowers: Linum (flax), monks hood, aconite

PLATE XL: 191. PILLOW, Hammersdorf; 192. PILLOW,
    Rumes; 193. PILLOW, Grossau;
    194. APRON, Mettersdorf; 195. APRON,
    Schönbirk

191) Greek crosses (counterchange) Sophisticated style
 Prototype: early Christian *(19th century)*
 Quaternity crosses
192) RAM (symbol of perseverance) at the tree of life
 Along a star of Bethlehem (mutilated style)
 (see also 77, 104, 115) *(18th century)*
193) Holy salver and feathered
 Tree of life Sophisticated
 Flower: Columbine (aquilegia) *(19th century style)*
 Lordly braid of faith, blessing ans health
 "S" health sign (brazen serpent, sign of social
 medicine)
194) Star of Bethlehem (quaternity cross) and the trinity
 (16th century)
195) Syrian scroll with pansy pattern *(18th century)*

BIBLIOGRAPHY

Banateanu, Fosca and Ionescu, Folk Costumes of Roumania. Bukarest 1958
H. Th. Bossert, Ornamente der Volkskunst. Tübingen 1949
N. A. Brodsky, L'Iconographie oubliée de l'Arc Ephésien de Sainte Marie Majeure à Rome. Bruxelles 1961
Buletinul Comisunii Monumentelor Istorice. Bucuresti 1923
Ciba Review I, Mediaeval Dyeing. Basle 1937
Colección Vinas, De Tejidos Antiguas Palacio de la Virreina. Barcelona 1957
Otto v. Falke, Decorative Silks. London 1922
Maurice H. Farbridge, Studies in Biblical and Semitic Symbolism. London 1923
Manuel Gomez-Moreno, Huelgas de Burgos. Madrid 1946
Donald Harden, The Phoenician. London 1962
A. G. L. Hellyer, Flowers in Colour. London 1960
Ernst Henri, Tapisseries et Etoffes Coptes. Paris
Holy Bible, Cambridge
Ali Hosain, Oriental Carpets. Braunschweig 1956
Renate Jaques, Mittelalterlicher Textildruck am Rhein. Kevelaer 1930
Pauline Johnstone, Greek Island Embroidery, London 1961
Heinz Edgar Kiewe, Forgotten Pictorial, Language of Israel. Paris 1951
Heinz Edgar Kiewe, Ancient Berber Tapestries & Rugs. Oxford 1952
Heinz Edgar Kiewe, Traditional Embroideries from the Holy Land and Norway. Oxford 1954
Heinz Edgar Kiewe, History of Folk Cross-stitch. Nürnberg 1962
Erich Kolbenheyer, Motive der hausindustriellen Stickerei in der Bukowina. Czernowitz 1912

Johann Kondert, Geschichte der Siebenbürger Sachsen. Munich 1955
Hanna Kronberger-Frentzen, Deutsche Stickmuster. Hamburg
Florence Lewis May, Silk Textiles of Spain. New York 1957
A. R. L. Milburn, Saints and their Emblems. Oxford 1957
F. van der Meer, Atlas of the early Christian World. London 1958
F. Meyer-Heisig, Weberci, Nadelwerk, Zeugdruck. München 1956
F. C. Norton, Information in the Study of Assyriology. Ditchling 1908
George Oprescu, Peasant Art in Roumania. London 1929
Giovanni Ostaus, La Vera Perfezione del Disegno per Punti e Ricami. Bergamo 1909
George Rawlinson, History of Phoenicia. London 1889
Hans Retzlaff, Die Siebenbürger Sachsen. Stuttgart 1959
Elisa Ricci, Trine Italiane Fascicolo Modano. Bergamo 1909
B. Rothemund, Byzantinische und russische Stickereien. München 1961
Elfriede Rottenbacher, Alpenlaendische Handarbeitsmuster. Graz 1956
M. Symonds and L. Preece, Needlework in Religion. London 1923
Giovanni Andrea Vavassore, Opera Nova Universal. Venice
Giovanni Andrea Vavassore, Esemplario di Cavori. Bergamo 1910
Frederico Vinciolo, I Singolari e Nuovi Disegni. Bergamo 1809
W. F. Volbach, Catalogo del Museo Sacro Vol. III i Tessuti. Citta del Vaticano 1942
W. F. Volbach, Early Christian Art. London 1961
Christian Zervos, L'art en Grece. London 1934
Heinrich Zillich, Siebenbürgen, ein abendländisches Schicksal. Königstein im Taunus 1957
H. Zillich, Siebenbürgisch-Sächsische Heimat-Fibel. München 1957

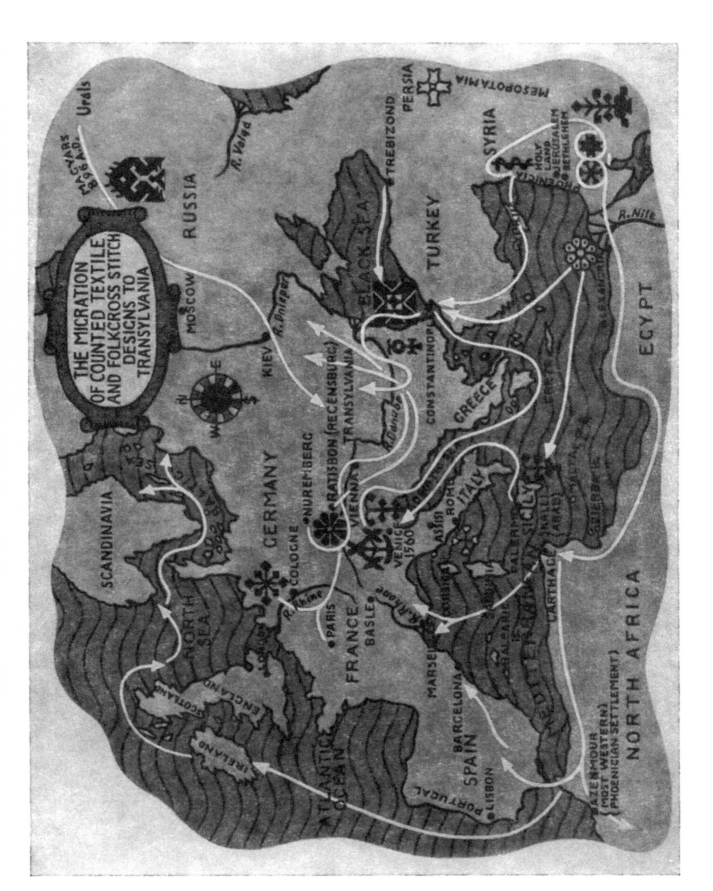

CHARTED PEASANT DESIGNS FROM SAXON TRANSYLVANIA

I

IV

VIII

XI

XII

XIII

XV

XVI

XVII

XVIII

XIX

XX

XXI

XXII

XXIV

XXV

XXVI

XXVIII

XXIX

XXXI

XXXIII

XXXIV

XXXV

XXXVI

XXXVII

XXXIX

XL